SPOTLIGHT ON THE CI

ROSA PARKS AND THE MONTGOMERY BUS BOYCOTT

ANITA LOUISE MCCORMICK

Rosen YA
New York

Published in 2018 by The Rosen Publishing Group, Inc.
29 East 21st Street, New York, NY 10010

Copyright © 2018 by The Rosen Publishing Group, Inc.

First Edition

All rights reserved. No part of this book may be reproduced in any form without permission in writing from the publisher, except by a reviewer.

Library of Congress Cataloging-in-Publication Data

Names: McCormick, Anita Louise, author.
Title: Rosa Parks and the Montgomery Bus Boycott / Anita Louise McCormick.
Description: New York, NY : Rosen Publishing Group, 2018. | Series: Spotlight on the Civil Rights Movement | Includes bibliographical references and index. | Audience: Grades 5–10.
Identifiers: LCCN 2017016921| ISBN 9781538380635 (library bound) | ISBN 9781538380628 (pbk.) | ISBN 9781538380611 (6 pack)
Subjects: LCSH: Parks, Rosa, 1913–2005—Juvenile literature. | Montgomery Bus Boycott, Montgomery, Ala., 1955–1956—Juvenile literature. | Civil rights—United States—History—Juvenile literature.
Classification: LCC F334.M753 P385543 2018 | DDC 323.092 [B]—dc23
LC record available at https://lccn.loc.gov/2017016921

Manufactured in the United States of America

On the cover: Rosa Parks faced jail, ridicule, job loss, and more to take a stand against racial discrimination in Montgomery, Alabama—in doing so, she inspired a nation to fight for civil rights.

CONTENTS

Rosa's Famous Bus Ride	4
Who Was Rosa Parks?	6
Early Experiences with Discrimination and the KKK	8
Civil Rights During the Early Twentieth Century	10
Rosa Parks Becomes Active in the Civil Rights Movement	12
African Americans and the Montgomery Bus System	14
Rosa Parks's Arrest	16
Rosa Parks Agrees to Challenge Unfair Laws	18
Planning a Response to Discrimination on Buses	20
Rosa Parks Is Found Guilty	22
The Montgomery Improvement Association	24
The Montgomery Bus Boycott	26
The City of Montgomery Fights Back	30
The Legal Process Moves Forward	32
Supreme Court Upholds Civil Rights	34
Moving On to a New Life in Detroit	36
Death and Funeral Services	38
Rosa Parks's Legacy	40
Glossary	42
For More Information	43
For Further Reading	45
Bibliography	46
Index	47

ROSA'S FAMOUS BUS RIDE

On December 1, 1955, Rosa Parks chose a seat on the Cleveland Avenue bus in Montgomery, Alabama. She was on her way home from her job as a seamstress at Montgomery Fair department store. Then, a white person boarded. The bus was nearly full and the driver ordered Parks and three other African American passengers to give up their seats. Parks did not think this was right. Even though African Americans paid the same fare as white passengers, they were only allowed to sit in seats behind a sign that said "colored." When the "whites only" section became full, African American passengers had to stand so white passengers could sit down. The other African American passengers reluctantly stood. But Rosa Parks did not get up.

Rosa Parks sits on a Montgomery city bus in front of a white passenger after her court victory.

She decided she'd had enough of being pushed around by an unfair system. The bus driver called the police and had Rosa Parks arrested. He thought that would be the end of the story. But it was only the beginning.

WHO WAS ROSA PARKS?

Rosa Louise McCauley was born on February 4, 1913, in Tuskegee, Alabama. She grew up in the small town of Pine Level, Alabama. Her mother was a school teacher, and her father built houses. When Rosa was young, her father went north to look for work. Rosa's mother took Rosa and her younger brother to live on her grandparents' farm. Rosa attended a rural one-room school for African American children. There was a better school nearby, but only white children were permitted to attend.

When Rosa was eleven, her mother enrolled her in the Montgomery Industrial School for Girls, a school founded by two white Christian education reformers from the Northeast. They wanted to help African American girls get a vocational and academic education during the time of segregation.

After that, Rosa went on to high school. But she had to leave school for a while to take care of her mother and later her grandmother when they became ill.

Rosa Parks grew up in this small wooden house in Pine Level, Alabama. Pine Level is located in Montgomery County, where the city of Montgomery is also located.

EARLY EXPERIENCES WITH DISCRIMINATION AND THE KKK

From an early age, Rosa Parks knew that African Americans were treated differently from white people. And if they did anything that might upset white people, their lives and property could be in danger.

She heard about threats from the Ku Klux Klan, or the KKK, against people in the African American community. She heard about lynchings, fire bombings, and other crimes the KKK committed. Her grandfather sometimes sat on the porch with a gun to protect his family in case the KKK came to attack them.

parade of the Klu-Klux Klan through countries in Virginia bordering on the District of Columbia, last night. 3/18/2

The Ku Klux Klan (KKK) held parades to show their strength and to intimidate African Americans.

Rosa learned from an early age that if she wanted to get along in the world, she had to be respectful toward white people, even if they were not respectful toward her. She knew the legal system had a double standard. African Americans could be beaten up or killed by white people and those responsible were often not charged or brought to justice.

CIVIL RIGHTS DURING THE EARLY TWENTIETH CENTURY

After the Civil War, many southern states passed Jim Crow laws that gave police and the courts legal power to enforce segregation between African Americans and whites.

African Americans were not permitted to use the same bathrooms, water fountains, and schools as white people. Facilities for whites were nearly always better than those for African Americans.

Even when African Americans were told they had a right to vote, local authorities found ways to prevent them from voting. Many polling stations would require African Americans to take tests, which white people were not required to take. Even when they passed, they could be told they failed.

At this time, anyone in the South who joined a civil rights organization such as the National Association for the Advancement of Colored People (NAACP) knew they were taking a big risk. White supremacists had threatened and fire bombed homes, churches, and civil rights organizations. They targeted anyone who was working to change Jim Crow laws.

This 1882 engraving, produced during the Jim Crow era, shows an African American man running from a white mob.

ROSA PARKS BECOMES ACTIVE IN THE CIVIL RIGHTS MOVEMENT

In 1932, Rosa married Raymond Parks, a barber who was active in the civil rights movement. Barber shops were often community gathering places. Because of this, Raymond Parks heard a lot about how African Americans in the area had been mistreated by whites, as well as the justice system.

In 1943, Rosa Parks attended her first meeting of the local NAACP. E. D. Nixon, who was the head of the organization, immediately asked Rosa to be the NAACP's secretary.

This 1936 photo of a laundry and barber shop shows an example of community gathering places of African Americans.

As part of her work, Parks researched stories of injustice against African Americans. She also helped raise money for their legal defense. Parks encouraged African Americans to register to vote, even if their requests were turned down multiple times. She also encouraged African Americans to attempt to check books out of libraries that were intended only for white people.

AFRICAN AMERICANS AND THE MONTGOMERY BUS SYSTEM

In the 1950s, about 75 percent of bus riders in Montgomery were African Americans. Few African Americans in the community were paid well enough to afford cars, so they often used public transportation instead of walking. But even though the fares from African American passengers kept the bus system going, they were treated like second-class citizens.

Having to sit in the "colored section" was not the only way the Montgomery bus system discriminated against African Americans. After they boarded the bus at the front to pay their fare, they had to get off the bus, walk to the back, and reboard there. Sometimes, bus drivers would take off before African American

Shown here is the restored bus Rosa Parks was riding in 1955 when she was arrested.

passengers who had paid their fare had time to walk to the back of the bus to reboard.

Bus drivers could be rude and unfair to African American passengers and nothing was done about it.

ROSA PARKS'S ARREST

When Parks was arrested for not giving up her seat on the bus, the news quickly spread throughout the community. Many people involved with the NAACP, African American churches, and the African American community in general were concerned about her safety. They did not want her to have to go to jail. When African American friends called the police station to find out what Rosa Parks had been charged with, they were treated rudely.

After a few hours, Rosa was permitted to call home. She let her husband, Raymond, know that she was charged with violating a city law requiring racial segregation of public buses. She also told him she was being held until $100 bail could be posted. This would be about $1,000 today. By the next day, her husband, E. D. Nixon, and some friends raised the money so she could be released.

Rosa Parks was arrested, booked, and photographed for not giving up her seat on the bus.

ROSA PARKS AGREES TO CHALLENGE UNFAIR LAWS

Before Rosa Parks's arrest, other African Americans had also been arrested for not giving up their seats on the bus. But for one reason or another, civil rights organizations did not think they could be used to challenge the law that permitted discrimination on city buses.

Rosa Parks was well known and respected in the community. Because of this, many people felt Parks's arrest would be an ideal case to challenge the law. They wanted to take the case all the way to the US Supreme Court if necessary. Parks did not really like the idea of being in the spotlight. She knew it would put her and

Many African American activists believed that the US Supreme Court offered the best hope for African Americans to gain equal rights.

her family in danger from the KKK. But she decided that changing the law was important enough to take the risk.

NAACP members, African American church leaders, and others who hoped to repeal Jim Crow laws began discussing what to do. Some white people in the community also wanted to help change these unfair laws.

PLANNING A RESPONSE TO DISCRIMINATION ON BUSES

Jo Ann Robinson, an African American professor who led the Women's Political Council, was one of the first people to suggest a bus boycott. The boycott was to happen on December 5, 1955, the day Rosa Parks was scheduled to appear in court. Many African American leaders in the Montgomery area agreed this would be a good way to protest the way they were being treated.

Once the decision had been made, word spread through the neighborhood that African Americans should stay off the Montgomery buses to protest segregation. E. D. Nixon called people

African American churches became a central rallying place for the Montgomery bus boycott.

in the community to let them know about the plans. Many African American church leaders were willing to help.

The Women's Political Council printed more than thirty-five thousand copies of a flyer announcing the boycott and gave them to as many people as possible. As a result, over 90 percent of African Americans in Montgomery stayed off the buses on December 5.

ROSA PARKS IS FOUND GUILTY

E. D. Nixon and the NAACP hired a lawyer, Fred Gray, to represent Rosa Parks in court. Gray was also an African American. Even with legal representation, the judge still found Rosa Parks guilty of breaking laws that enforced segregation. She was fined fourteen dollars. When the hearing was over, Fred Gray stated that Parks would not pay the fine because she had done nothing wrong. He also said he would take her case all the way to the Supreme Court if necessary.

As word about this decision went through the African American community in Montgomery, many people became more determined than ever to support the appeal.

In a previous case, *Brown v. Board of Education*, the Supreme Court had ruled that segregation of schools was against the Constitution and therefore illegal. So if school segregation was illegal, how could it be legal to have segregation on public buses?

Fred Gray, who represented Rosa Parks in court, was both a minister and a lawyer. He studied for his law degree in Ohio because no law school in Alabama admitted African Americans.

THE MONTGOMERY IMPROVEMENT ASSOCIATION

At first, the African American community was only planning to boycott the buses for one day. But after the charges against Rosa Parks were not dropped, they decided not to ride the buses again until the law was changed. Since 75 percent of bus riders were African American, the boycott made running buses unprofitable. The NAACP and African American church leaders decided to form a new group called the Montgomery Improvement Association to work for change. E. D. Nixon, the president of the NAACP, was elected as the treasurer. The organization was founded on the idea of working for change through nonviolence.

Civil rights leader Reverend Martin Luther King Jr. rides on a Montgomery city bus after the segregation laws had been repealed.

African American churches were important gathering places for people who wanted to end segregation. Martin Luther King Jr. was a new, young minister in the area. Many people came to listen to him speak.

Because of King's rapidly rising popularity, the Montgomery Improvement Association decided to elect him as the leader of their organization.

THE MONTGOMERY BUS BOYCOTT

By this time, most African Americans were fully committed to staying off the city buses until they were given the same rights as white passengers. Instead of riding the bus, most African Americans in Montgomery walked or formed carpools. African American cab drivers lowered their fees to a dime so people who had been riding the bus could afford their service.

African American churches, the NAACP, and other community groups helped organize the carpools. Nearly three hundred people made their cars available to help with the boycott. Some white employers who supported an end to segregation gave their African American employees rides.

City officials and bus company officials assumed that African Americans would soon grow tired of walking and organizing carpools and go back to riding the buses. But that did not happen.

For over a year, hardly any African Americans rode city buses.

This sign marks the bus stop on Dexter Avenue in Montgomery, Alabama, where Rosa Parks waited for the bus on the day of her arrest.

27

Rosa Parks worked as a seamstress at the Montgomery Fair department store. Later, she lost her job due to her involvement with the boycott.

While the Montgomery bus boycott was working, some African Americans found they had to pay a heavy price for their involvement. Rosa Parks lost her job as a seamstress at the department store because they did not want to deal with the controversy. Other people lost their jobs for being involved with the boycott or assisting people who needed rides.

The KKK, White Citizens Council, and others who did not want to see segregation end constantly harassed and made threats against people who supported the boycott. Rosa Parks, her husband, Martin Luther King Jr., E. D. Nixon, and many other African American church leaders and NAACP members and supporters received threatening phone calls throughout the boycott. The homes of Martin Luther King Jr., E. D. Nixon, and other civil rights leaders were damaged by firebombs.

THE CITY OF MONTGOMERY FIGHTS BACK

The city of Montgomery and the bus company thought the boycott would be over quickly. They did not think African Americans would be able to stay off the buses for so long. Every day the boycott went on, the bus system lost money. Even some white passengers were staying off the bus in support of ending segregation.

To retaliate, in February 1956, the city of Montgomery declared the boycott illegal. Montgomery police started arresting people for being involved with the boycott. They also harassed and ticketed carpool drivers.

Nearly one hundred people were arrested for organizing and participating in the boycott. Rosa Parks was arrested. The police took a mug shot and her fingerprints. They also arrested E. D. Nixon, Jo Ann Robinson, Fred Gray, and many other boycotters.

Rosa Parks was arrested and fingerprinted for her role in the Montgomery bus boycott.

Martin Luther King Jr. was arrested and fined for leading the boycott. He went to jail for two weeks for refusing to pay the $500 fine. But no matter what the city, bus company, or even the KKK did, the bus boycott continued.

THE LEGAL PROCESS MOVES FORWARD

While the city of Montgomery and the bus company were doing everything they could to try to stop the boycott, civil rights lawyers were working to advance the case to the highest court in the nation. The Supreme Court had ruled against Jim Crow laws before, so taking their case to the Supreme Court appeared to be the best path to victory.

During this time, newspapers, TV, and radio stations all over the world reported on the Montgomery, Alabama, bus boycott. This helped the movement gain even more support. Supporters helped by sending money for legal expenses and gasoline. Some people donated shoes for people who had to walk to work.

On June 5, 1956, the Montgomery Federal Court ruled that laws requiring segregation on buses were unconstitutional. The city of Montgomery appealed and the case then went to the Supreme Court.

The Montgomery bus boycott made headlines in the local newspaper and in newspapers all across the country.

SUPREME COURT UPHOLDS CIVIL RIGHTS

On November 13, 1956, the Supreme Court upheld the federal court's decision ruling that segregation on public buses was unconstitutional. Then, on December 20, 1956, the Supreme Court delivered a written order to Montgomery government officials stating that segregation on public buses would no longer be tolerated.

African Americans in Montgomery started riding the buses again. The boycott had lasted for 381 days. Rosa Parks had her photo taken while sitting in a bus seat that had once been reserved for white passengers.

The success of this action proved once again that injustice against African Americans could be successfully challenged in court. It also brought Martin Luther King Jr. into the news as an important civil rights leader.

After the Supreme Court ruling outlawing segregation on public transportation, African Americans started to ride Montgomery buses again.

But shortly after the decision, the KKK bombed four black churches and the homes of African American leaders. They also fired guns into buses. The arrest of seven KKK members involved with the crimes helped stop the violence.

35

MOVING ON TO A NEW LIFE IN DETROIT

After the bus boycott was over, Parks was unable to find work. She and her husband moved to Detroit, Michigan, where she worked as a seamstress until she was hired by US representative John Conyers to work on his staff.

In 1987, as a way of helping her community, Rosa and her husband started the Rosa and Raymond Parks Institute for Self Development. The institute helps black students continue with their education and find meaningful careers. The organization also works to encourage young people to become involved in their communities and learn about the history of the civil rights movement.

Rosa Parks and US Congressman John Conyers Jr. protest in front of General Motors corporate headquarters in Detroit, Michigan.

In her later years, Rosa Parks made many public appearances to speak about civil rights and other causes that were important to her. In 1992, Rosa Parks wrote an autobiography for young readers, *Rosa Parks: My Story*. She also wrote a book sharing letters young people had written to her over the years.

DEATH AND FUNERAL SERVICES

On October 24, 2005, Rosa Parks died of natural causes in her Detroit apartment at the age of ninety-two. Because of Rosa Parks's important contributions to the civil rights movement, people in many parts of the country wanted to honor her after her passing. Her coffin was flown to Montgomery, Alabama, and taken by horse-drawn carriage to the St. Paul African Methodist Episcopal Church. Many famous people came to pay their respects. Thousands of ordinary people came, too.

After the funeral service, Rosa Parks's coffin was flown to Washington, DC. She was the first woman and second African American to lie in state in the rotunda of the US Capitol. More than thirty thousand people passed by her casket. A service was then held at the Metropolitan African Methodist Episcopal Church in Washington, DC. There was also a funeral service for her in Detroit, Michigan. The church was packed with nearly four thousand people who wanted to honor her. Rosa Parks was buried on November 2, 2005, at Woodlawn Cemetery in Detroit, Michigan.

Civil rights activist Rosa Parks lies in state in the Rotunda of the Capitol Building in Washington, DC.

ROSA PARKS'S LEGACY

Rosa Parks has been honored in many different ways for her work as a civil rights leader.

There is a Rosa Parks Library and Museum at Troy University in Montgomery, Alabama, where people can learn about her life and work to help African Americans gain equal rights.

In 1996, Rosa Parks received a Presidential Medal of Freedom from President Bill Clinton. The medal has a picture of her on the center. The inscription around the outside of the medal says, "Mother of the Modern Day Civil Rights Movement."

Even after her death, Rosa Parks continues to receive honors for her work. In 2013, the year that would have marked Rosa Parks's one hundredth birthday, a US postage stamp was issued in her honor. In this same year, she was also the first African American woman to be honored with a statue in the US Capitol's Statuary Hall. It was unveiled by Barack Obama, the first African American president of the United States.

Rosa Parks at the White House after receiving the 1996 Presidential Medal of Freedom in Washington, DC, from President Bill Clinton.

GLOSSARY

boycott Protesting by refusing to buy a product or use a service.

carpool A means of transportation where people use a car to share rides.

civil disobedience Disobeying laws that are unfair or holding protests not allowed by government leaders.

civil rights The rights of all citizens to be treated equally and have equal rights and government protection under the law.

civil rights movement A movement of organizations and individuals who worked for equal rights for all citizens.

colored A word that was once commonly used to refer to African Americans.

fire bomb A homemade bomb the KKK made that was intended to destroy buildings and hurt or kill those inside.

Jim Crow laws Laws that were passed to legally enforce discrimination, such as laws that required African Americans to use different schools, water fountains, and bathrooms than white people.

Ku Klux Klan (KKK) A white supremacist group that used threats and violence to oppose civil rights.

lynch The mob killing of a person without giving him or her a trial, usually by hanging.

National Association for the Advancement of Colored People (NAACP) An organization that was founded to help African Americans and other nonwhite people have equal rights and protection under the law.

seamstress A person who sews or repairs and resizes clothes.

segregation Laws or policies that required African Americans to use different schools, bathrooms, drinking fountains, and other facilities than whites.

voting rights The right to take part in registering to vote and voting to elect government officials.

FOR MORE INFORMATION

Black History in Canada
The 2Learn.ca Education Society
15120 104 Ave NW
Edmonton, AB T5P 0R5
Canada
(780) 486-0380
Website: http://www.2learn.ca/enjoy/blackhistory
Facebook: @2Learn.ca
Twitter: @2Learn_ca
An organization that helps to promote technology-enriched teaching and learning in partnership with community organizations.

National Association for the Advancement of Colored People (NAACP)
National Headquarters
4805 Mt. Hope Drive
Baltimore, MD 21215
(877) NAACP-98
Website: http://naacp.org
Facebook: @naacp
Twitter: @NAACP
Instagram: @naacp
One of the nation's oldest and largest grassroots civil rights organizations. It works for educational, political, and economic equality of all people.

Rosa and Raymond Parks Institute
535 Griswold, Suite 111/513
Detroit, MI 48226
(313) 965-0606
Website: http://rosaparks.org

Facebook: @Rosa-and-Raymond-Parks-Institute-for-Self-Development
/11598528029
Twitter: @RRPI535
Instagram: @ROSA.RAYMOND_PARKS_INSTITUTE
Rosa and Raymond Parks set up this organization to carry on their work for youth development and civil rights advocacy.

Rosa Parks Museum at Troy University
231 Montgomery Street
Montgomery, AL 36104
(334) 241-8615
Website: http://www.troy.edu/rosaparks
Email: rosaparks@troy.edu
Facebook: @TroyUniversityRosaParksMuseum
Twitter: @RosaParksMuseum
Instagram: @rosaparksmuseum
A museum that was created to collect and make available for public use and enjoyment, materials related to the events and accomplishments of Rosa Parks and others associated with the Montgomery bus boycott.

WEBSITES

Because of the changing nature of internet links, Rosen Publishing has developed an online list of websites related to the subject of this book. This site is updated regularly. Please use this link to access this list:

http://www.rosenlinks.com/SCRM/Parks

FOR FURTHER READING

Aretha, David. *The Story of Rosa Parks and the Montgomery Bus Boycott in Photographs*. New York, NY: Enslow Publishing, 2014.

Eaddy, Michael. *E. D. Nixon: The Unsung Father of the Montgomery Bus Boycott*. New York, NY: MEaddyWorks, 2016.

Gitlin, Martin. *The Montgomery Bus Boycott: A History Perspectives Book*. North Mankato, MN: Cherry Lake Publishing, 2013.

Hare, Kenneth M., *They Walked to Freedom 1955–1956*. Champaign, IL: Spotlight Press, L.L.C, 2005.

Kenney, Karen Latchana. *Rosa Parks and the Montgomery Bus Boycott*. Minneapolis, MN: Core Library, 2015.

Kimmel, Allison Crotzer. *The Montgomery Bus Boycott: A Primary Source Exploration of the Protest for Equal Treatment*. Mankato, MN: Capstone Press, 2015.

Mahoney, Emily. *American Civil Rights Movement*. New York, NY: Rosen Publishing, 2017.

Miller, Connie Colwell, *Rosa Parks and the Montgomery Bus Boycott*. Mankato, MN: Capstone Press, 2006.

Parks, Rosa. *Dear Mrs. Parks: A Dialogue with Today's Youth*. New York, NY: Lee & Low Books, 1996.

Reynolds, Toby. *Fearless Women: Courageous Females Who Refused to be Denied*. Hauppauge, NY: Barron's Educational Series, 2017.

BIBLIOGRAPHY

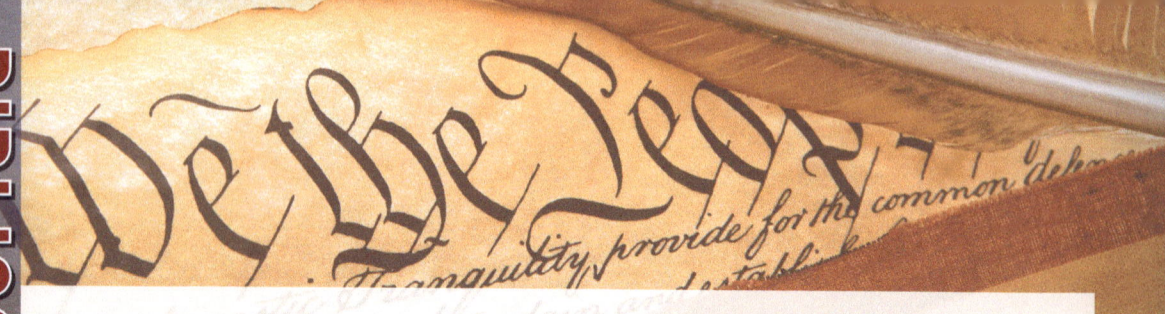

Brinkley, Douglas, *Rosa Parks*. New York, NY: Penguin Lives, 2000.

Hare, Kenneth M. *They Walked to Freedom 1955–1956*. Champaign, IL: Spotlight Press, L.L.C, 2005.

Kellaher, Karen, and the editors of *Time for Kids*. *Rosa Parks, Civil Rights Pioneer*. New York, NY: HarperCollins Publishing, 2007.

Keys, Sheila McCauley. *Our Auntie Rosa: The Family of Rosa Parks Remembers Her Life and Lessons*. New York, NY: TarcherPerigee/Penguin, 2015.

"Parks, Rosa (1913–2005)." The King Institute. Retrieved March 5, 2017. http://kingencyclopedia.stanford.edu/encyclopedia/encyclopedia/enc_parks_rosa_1913_2005.

Parks, Rosa, and Gregory J. Reed. *Quiet Strength: The Faith, the Hope, and the Heart of a Woman Who Changed a Nation*. Grand Rapids, MI: Zondervan Publishing House, 1994.

Robinson, Jo Ann Gibson. *The Montgomery Bus Boycott and the Women Who Started It*. Knoxville, TN: University of Tennessee Press, 1987.

Rothman, Lilly. "Listen to a Rare Recording of Rosa Parks Telling Her Story." *Time*. January 21, 2016. http://time.com/4187961/rosa-parks-studs-terkel.

Schmitz, Paul. "How Change Happens: The Real Story of Mrs. Rosa Parks & The Montgomery Bus Boycott." December 1, 2014. http://www.huffingtonpost.com/paul-schmitz/how-change-happens-the-re_b_6237544.html.

Theoharis, Jeanne. *The Rebellious Life of Mrs. Rosa Parks*. Boston, MA: Beacon Press, 2013.

INDEX

A
arrest, 5, 16, 18, 30

B
boycott, 20–21, 24, 26, 29–32, 34, 36
Brown v. Board of Education, 22

C
childhood, 6
civil rights, 10, 11, 18, 29, 32, 34, 37, 40
civil rights movement, 12, 36, 38, 40
Civil War, 10
Clinton, Bill, 40
Conyers, John, 36

D
death, 38–39

E
education, 6, 36

G
Gray, Fred, 22, 30

J
Jim Crow laws, 10–11, 19, 32

K
King, Martin Luther Jr., 25, 29, 31, 34
Ku Klux Klan, 8, 19, 29, 31, 35

M
Medal of Freedom, 40
Metropolitan African Methodist Episcopal Church, 39
Montgomery Federal Court, 32
Montgomery Improvement Association, 24–25
Montgomery Industrial School for Girls, 6

N
National Association for the Advancement of Colored People (NAACP), 10, 12, 16, 19, 22, 24, 26, 29
Nixon, E. D., 12, 16, 20, 22, 24, 29, 30
nonviolence, 24

O
Obama, Barack, 40

P
Parks, Raymond, 12, 16, 36
postage stamp, 40

R
Robinson, Jo Ann, 20, 30
Rosa and Raymond Parks Institute for Self Development, 36
Rosa Parks Library and Museum, 40
Rosa Parks: My Story, 37

S
segregation, 6, 10, 16, 20, 22, 25, 25, 29, 30, 32, 34
St. Paul African Methodist Episcopal Church, 38
Statuary Hall, 40
Supreme Court, 18, 22, 32, 34

V
voting rights, 10

W
White Citizens Council, 29
white supremacists, 11
Women's Political Council, 20–21

About the Author

Anita Louise McCormick is a longtime author who enjoys writing about her many interests, including American history and the civil rights movement. Her books include *The Native American Struggle in United States History*, *The Vietnam Antiwar Movement in American History*, and *The Industrial Revolution in United States History*.

Photo Credits

Cover, p. 1 Donaldson Collection/Michael Ochs Archives/Getty Images; pp. 3, 42, 43, 45, 46, 47 Onur Ersin/Shutterstock.com; pp. 4, 6, 8, 10, 12, 14, 16, 18, 20, 22, 24, 26, 30, 32, 34, 36, 38, 40, back cover Sergey Kamshylin/Shutterstock.com; pp. 5, 31 Underwood Archives/Archive Photos/Getty Images; p. 7 The Washington Post/Getty Images; pp. 9, 27 Library of Congress Prints and Photographs Division; pp. 11, 13 Everett Historical/Shutterstock.com; p. 15 Joseph Sohm/Shutterstock.com; p. 17 Universal Images Group/Getty Images; p. 19 Orhan Cam/Shutterstock.com; pp. 21, 23, 28–29, 33, 35 Don Cravens/The LIFE Images Collection/Getty Images; p. 25 Bettmann/Getty Images; p. 37 Tom Williams/CQ-Roll Call Group/Getty Images; p. 39 Chris Maddaloni/CQ-Roll Call Group/Getty Images; p. 41 Richard Ellis/AFP/Getty Images.

Design: Nelson Sá; Editor and Photo Researcher: Xina M. Uhl